To MIKE!

WARM regards to
A fellow TRAVELER..

Daybreak in Myanmar

Geoffrey Hiller

www.hillerphoto.com

To Linda

Daybreak in Myanmar

PHOTOGRAPHS BY GEOFFREY HILLER

Contents

Foreword

Journalist Francis Wade

Most people alive in Burma today will know little of life outside of military rule. That era, if it can yet be confined to the past, has sculpted much of what is visible in the country today: the neglect of Yangon's architecture, a once beautiful if audacious illustration of Britain's colonial designs that has been left to crumble into the streets; the austere new capital of Naypyidaw, planned and executed at vast expense on the advice of a fortune teller, and occupied by a paranoid clique of army generals. These and myriad other symbols mark a half-century period in which the country withdrew from the world. For some, behind this decay lies a poignant reminder of what could have been, had the country's brief flirtation with democracy after independence in 1948 endured; others will find the anguish intensely personal, with millions of lives and livelihoods lost. Still more will see Burma in its present state as a land of vast and untapped potential, whose opening is cause for great excitement. Both ends of the spectrum are crowded.

As I write, Burma is slowly and painfully emerging from the darkness and into an age of cautious optimism, but also anxiety. Life following the coup of 1962 that began military rule was often harsh and unyielding—tens of thousands of dissidents were jailed, rural populations were uprooted as the army sought to control the borderlands, and economic hardships seeped into every aspect of day-to-day living. Yet life was perversely simple: routines were regimented, emotions were muted and creativity was stifled. In a sense, people knew where they stood. With the game now changing, once-disenfranchised citizens are gaining a degree of control over their lives and their country that many have never experienced.

The images in this book span a period of more than 25 years beginning with Geoffrey Hiller's first visit to Burma in 1987. A year later, Aung San Suu Kyi returned to Burma, and quickly began articulating a vision of the country's future distinct from the picture drawn over nearly four decades by the military. The subsequent resignation of General Ne Win, Burma's first dictator, sparked mass protests in pursuit of democracy that swept towns and cities the length of the country. The army moved in, and up to 6,000 people died. But rather than heralding change, the generals jailed Suu Kyi, annulled her party's victory in the 1990 elections and hardened their rule. History appeared to repeat itself in 2007 when a monk-led uprising, later dubbed the Saffron Revolution, ended in a bloody crackdown.

What can photography tell us about those intervening years, when the veil, momentarily lifted in 1988, was drawn back over Burma? It can tell us that the aesthetics of the country changed little. A gleaming if sterile new capital may have opened in 2006, but for the average citizen in Yangon, in Mandalay, in the towns and villages from Chin state to Karen state, from Putao to Kawthaung, time largely stood still. In the more remote areas of the country, where outsiders seldom tread and where villages are yet to be electrified, life remains much the same as it did a century ago. The lack of change across Hiller's images of this period stands as a powerful indictment of the nature of dictatorial rule and its imperviousness to evolution. But importantly, this body of work also demonstrates that the journalism industry's persistent eagerness to cast Burmese as an oppressed population sapped of the joys of life is false. Rather, Hiller catches the dignity and unflinching stoicism that have been their chief mechanisms of survival.

The latest chapter in Burma's story is harder to render in pictures. Yangon's streets may be gridlocked by new cars, and newspaper stands may tout a freer press — all signs of progress that must be applauded — but these surface changes belie a reluctance on the part of the country's elite, a shady and powerful nexus of military, political and business figures, to relinquish their grip on the country's affairs. In the border regions, the army continues its campaign of subordination — some say 'Burmanization' — of ethnic minority groups in an effort to unite the country under "one flag", and jail cells remain the activist's last stand, with ambiguous laws in force that still criminalize freedom of expression. Perhaps the saddest by-product of this hoped-for passage to democracy is the spread of conflict between Buddhists and Muslims, with the latter depicted as a threat to Burmese society and its sacred Buddhist institutions, and targeted with a vicious and sustained campaign of violence.

Beyond all this lies the delicate and mesmerizing beauty of the country, a diverse land of jungles, mist-raked mountains, cities and temple-studded plains, whose people have weathered the harshest of storms. Any visitor to these pages will note the resilience of the subjects, a sight that must be contrasted with the fact that many of these images were taken prior to the beginning of Burma's opening in early 2011, when state repression was often suffocating. As that era recedes into history, the indelible marks it has left behind, both good and bad, must be factored into any narrative that develops around the new Burma, in order that the country's collective memory remains intact and the past helps guide the future. We hope these photographs will make at least a small contribution towards this.

Introduction

PHOTOGRAPHER GEOFFREY HILLER

I grew up in New York, so it's always been on crowded city streets where I have felt most at home. Since my teenage years photography has helped me make sense of the world. When I walk the streets of a place like Burma, the adrenalin kicks in and my 'hungry eye' takes over. By framing the place, it's as if I'm reinventing the world.

Part of the process involves putting myself in the right state of mind. It begins before the sunrise when I wake up to catch the best light, heading toward wherever the pulse of the place might be. It becomes visceral, to find that one image that expresses the feeling of the place.

I use my intuition in each particular instance; sometimes it takes sitting down in a tea shop and waiting for a gesture and then the photograph can happen. It's ironic that in a place as repressive as Myanmar, the Burmese often accepted my presence and allowed me to photograph them.

I first visited the country in 1987 when it was still 'Burma' (the military government later changed the name to 'Myanmar') on the standard one-week visa. After a frenetic trip to Yangon, Mandalay and the temples of Bagan, it wasn't so much the monks and pagodas that haunted me, but the faces of the Burmese, painted in traditional white thanaka. I remember speaking with a few elderly professors but no one else was able to speak English, since the dictatorship that seized power in 1962 had isolated the country from the outside world. The travel restrictions were frustrating, but I vowed to go back.

That was before the pro-democracy uprising in 1988, the election of Aung San Suu Kyi a year later and the bloody crackdown by the generals and then her years-long house arrest. After more student-led protests in the 1990's, many Western countries signed onto economic sanctions, which further isolated Burma.

Despite the travel boycott, I returned in 2000. I was permitted to stay longer and travel more freely, in Pathein, Hpa-An and Mawlamyine. The military was still restrictive, however, so I had to go undercover and hide my cameras. There were times when I knew I was being followed by government spies, and more than once I was stopped and interrogated by plainclothes agents, in tea shops and in the street. It was a miracle that I was able to exit the country with 90 rolls of exposed film. The result was the web documentary "Burma: Grace Under Pressure."

In the following years things went from bad to worse, leading up to the monk-led protests of the Saffron Revolution which were violently put down in 2007, resulting in more deaths and more political prisoners. Months later Cyclone Nargis devastated the delta, and foreign ships carrying aid were not allowed to land on Burmese shores.

Fast forward to 2011, after I had spent a year teaching on a Fulbright grant in Bangladesh, when the United States Embassy hired me to teach photojournalists in Yangon. This seemed unbelievable, as I got on the plane that May with a tourist visa, worried that my name might be on a blacklist at customs. Little did anyone know that by the end of that year, the government was going to relax censorship and begin opening up to the outside world. Still I didn't see one single picture of 'The Lady', Nobel laureate Aung San Suu Kyi, anywhere. The students in my classes joked about how in Burma they didn't so much 'point and shoot' with their cameras, but had to 'point and run'. It was out of the question for me to take these students out to photograph in the streets, as I had done in other countries in South Asia.

By early 2012, Hillary Clinton made her historic visit. It was monumental to witness one of the first rallies where Aung San Suu Kyi and her National League for Democracy (NLD) party were allowed to campaign in public. I was now able to meet openly in public with my former students, who helped me set up interviews at events such as the initial release of hundreds of political prisoners. The mood on the streets of Yangon was exuberant, but I kept wondering how much things would really change for the vast majority who lived in the impoverished villages.

In 2013 I focused on capturing life in smaller towns that were formerly off-limits to foreigners. In February, just weeks before fighting erupted between Buddhists and Muslims, I stayed in Meiktila, a town I described soon afterward to the Irrawaddy News as 'peaceful.' I had spent time drinking tea in the Muslim tea shops, where people were welcoming and friendly. Later, I could not believe it when I read the news accounts of the horrible aftermath, with dozens of deaths and tens of thousands of Muslims displaced. Re-editing the photographs a year later for this book, I clearly saw the tension that was present.

As I write now in 2014 it's amazing that some of my former students are working for national and international media organizations and traveling unrestricted (for now) using smartphones and posting their photos to Facebook and Twitter. The landscape has changed, but as the Burmese in the interviews here clearly show, there is a lot of uncertainty going forward.

Dawn

အာရုံး

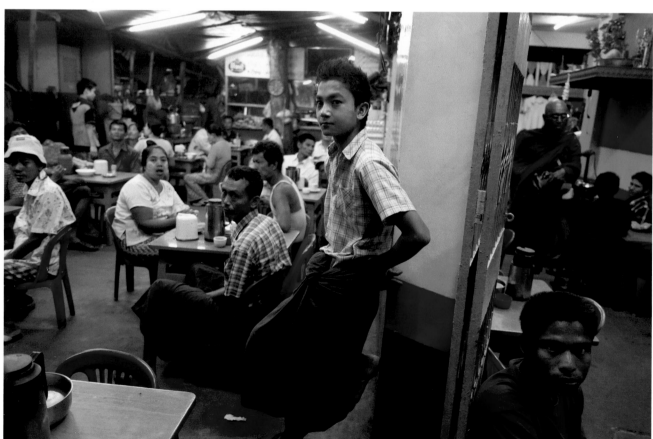

Thant Myint U

ON PRESERVING YANGON'S HISTORY

Thant Myint U, the grandson of former UN Secretary General U Thant, was born in New York and studied history at Harvard and Cambridge universities. His two most notable books, *The River of Lost Footsteps* and *Where China Meets India*, chart the history and political development of Burma up to the modern day. He founded the Yangon Heritage Trust in 2011, and the following year was named one of Foreign Policy Magazine's 100 Leading Global Thinkers.

Efforts to conserve Yangon's heritage have attracted support from all corners. There's evidently a common desire to keep the city's history alive.

I spent about a month here nearly every year after my first visit aged eight. The city back then was much less crowded and its early 20th century landscape was completely intact. I remember even back in the 1980s thinking how beautiful it was, the views of the Shwedagon but also the tree-lined avenues (there were many more trees then) and the boulevards downtown. The buildings then were all built for this environment, with big verandahs and porticos for the rainy season, and very little air-conditioning required. It was of course a much more isolated city and I think a much less materialistic one, with almost everyone equally poor, for better or worse.

The city has real historical significance in Burma and beyond.

It's internationally significant as a city that was once one of the most important ports of the British Empire and Asia, as a battleground during WW2, and as a uniquely cosmopolitan place, the place for which the term 'plural society' was first invented. For the Burmese it's more. It's where the Burmese first connected with the outside world, listened to jazz, read Sigmund Freud and Karl Marx, watched Hollywood movies, and debated Cold War foreign policy. It's the home of Burma's liberal as well as democratic traditions. If we erase the physical reminders of that earlier age, we weaken all our connections with the men and women who first embraced a more liberal way of life.

Do you worry that the 21ˢᵗ century will take its toll on Burma's heritage?

Yangon is at a turning point. It can either become an ungovernable urban sprawl with huge income inequalities and social tensions or one of the most beautiful and livable cities in Asia, attracting skills and creative talent, an engine for the growth of the entire economy. It's impossible to say right now which way things will go. Myanmar's been open for two decades; with the end of Western sanctions the only difference is the growth of Western interest and potential investment. And over these two decades a certain political economy has developed, one that has led to increasing inequality and a large portion of people completely left behind. What we're seeing now is the further integration of Myanmar into global markets. Whether it can develop the institutions to manage that integration in the way that benefits the majority and protects the most vulnerable remains to be seen.

Certain buildings mean radically different things to Burmese—Pegu Club, in which Kipling et al wined and dined, and the Secretariat, for example—but all need preserving.

The Pegu Club was a symbol of colonial exclusion and domination. It's important historically. The Secretariat was for a few decades the center of colonial administration but then was the center of Burmese government and Burmese democracy for many years. It's where Burmese democracy was born. It was also where some of the key moments in the country's history took place, not least the assassination of General Aung San and his cabinet in 1947. Our future will be a lot poorer without these physical links to the past. Having been a center of colonial and then later military administrations, I think it would be wonderful if in its newest incarnation the Secretariat would become something open to all people. It could have shops and offices but also public event spaces, for concerts and exhibitions, lectures and other public gatherings.

In this city you can chart the history of Burma from pre-modern times to now. The buildings can be used as educational tools, but there's always that question of whether the government is ready to lift the lid on the recent past.

It's not just changing the way the history of the post-1962 period is taught, but all history. I think students should be taught a much more critical view of history, one that appreciates the many different narratives that exist, including from ethnic and religious minorities, and learn to question the dominant nationalist narrative that's part of nearly everything people are taught (to the extent they are taught any history). A particularly narrow ethnic-based nationalism I've always argued is at the heart of many of the country's ills, not just since 1962.

Could these developments unnerve Yangon residents?

It will take years before most people are in a position to really appreciate the city's built heritage and value what we have. But if we don't do anything about it now, by then it will be too late. This is the story of nearly all other major Asian cities. In the early days of growth, no one cares, then when people really want to keep their old cityscapes, it's too late. That's what I want to avoid: Yangon waking up one day and realizing it has lost a beautiful city.

Early Morning

နံနက်ခင်း

54

Pascal Khoo Thwe

On Life in the Borderlands

Pascal Khoo Thwe grew up on the western shore of Inle Lake, across from the sprawl of upmarket resorts, in the town of Pekong. His chance encounter with Cambridge don Dr John Casey at Mandalay University in the late 1980s led to his enrollment at Cambridge University and immersion in a literary scene he has never left. Pascal's award-winning book, *From The Land of Green Ghosts*, details his childhood in the Padaung tribe and journey from his remote home in Shan State to the United Kingdom.

Your childhood in Pekong must have left you with some vivid and indelible memories.

Being close to nature was one thing I remember most. Going to farms, looking for food, coming home and eating the food we collected. Food and other materials were quite scarce and I remember being hungry all the time. We had rice and meat but not much, but we could just go into the lake and catch fish. Or we'd go into the jungle when we felt like eating wild animals and hunt them with catapults or bows and arrows, or dig up moles and bring them home and cook them. The noise of animals and human beings is something I remember strongly — chickens crowing, cows mooing, insects and birds. And seasonal noises — frogs in the rainy season, and so on; the smells of rains coming, and the smell of the dust.

A rich background that must have stoked your passion for literature and the arts...

Oral tradition was strong in the town. So we listened to the stories of our grandparents and mothers, or went to the church where bible stories became a part of our literary diet. There was a strong culture of storytelling and singing the tribal songs of our ancestors. When you visited other communities they would tell you stories about their lives. Village cultures across the country have this tradition, but it varies — the Shan, for instance, would tell their life story through song; the Karen tradition is more spoken, similar to ours because we are cousin tribes.

Did the regime try to stifle imagination among the people?

There were traditions but in those days they were much more organic. After the military coup, the regime sought to control this vibrancy in the same way the Soviets or Nazis did in order to create a definite Myanmar identity. That's when it started to go wrong. But I think the biggest damage they've done is to stifle the imaginative strength of their people. So there isn't that liveliness that there used to be in so-called traditional Myanmar music or art; more recent architectural styles are more for marketing, and not expression. This became more obvious after the 1962 coup. The aesthetic lost its sense of adventure.

How integral were spirits and religion to the construction of your society?

Religious beliefs tend to come about from two major causes. One is oppression — people take solace in it. The other is poverty, and poverty can cause anyone to believe in religion. Even before the arrival of Buddhism in our area the tribes were animist — spirit worshippers. Our tribal tradition goes all the way back to Mongolia, Tibet and even South America — our traditions of animal sacrifice, pattern weaving and shamanism are quite similar, and these were passed down from generation to generation. Buddhism was brought to our area maybe 200 or 300 years ago by the Shan and the Burman, and then Christian missionaries came 100 or 150 years ago. I belong to the Catholic Church but also hold animist beliefs — the line is quite thin.

Are once disparate tribes gradually coming together as Burma moves forward?

In my family's quarters in Pekong you have Catholics and Buddhists and sub-categories of Buddhists, Padaung and Inthar tribes and so on, living cheek by jowl. There are two villages near my town divided only by a hedge. They're of the same race but they speak two different dialects, and you can identify which side of the hedge they're from by the way they speak. I'm trying to collect dialects, because behind them are many stories. My grandfather's village had one dialect and my grandmother's another dialect; by the time we were born, a completely new dialect had emerged, mixing the two. Already however we're losing these old traditions — my nieces and nephews don't speak Padaung, they speak Burmese, and it's a conscious decision by the government to homogenize or 'Burmanize' these areas, to wipe out these ethnic identities. In school, children are made to feel ashamed of their tribal backgrounds — they'll say, 'Oh you're Padaung tribe, you'll have no chance to use your language to get a job or whatever'. The campaign is less intense now but the damage has been done.

The roots of this animosity between central Burma and ethnic minority groups are complicated and sad.

It goes a long way back, and has racial and nationalistic elements, the latter which have changed over the past century. Most ethnic groups don't know how the central government works, apart from the police and military in their hometowns. Nobody understands why they need a central government. For the tribesmen, the Burma army and Burmese nationalism are the same thing, so when we talk about the Bamar, the first thing we see is the army — they are the ambassadors of nationalism in the ethnic areas. That's the post-war version of nationalism. The Burmese kings were hated but they didn't really shout in your face the way the governments since 1962 have. After the war, Burmese rulers felt so hurt by colonialism that they had to find some scapegoat for their anger.

Burmese people are more passive than the rulers, but they still want an aspiring Burman ruler like Aung San Suu Kyi. But groups like the Mon and the Shan know that their culture is older than the Burman and they are angry because they know certain aspects of Burman culture were stolen from them. Once the oppression was intensified, both sides tried to exonerate their cause by creating legends or claiming lands, and so I take both Burman and my own tribe's nationalism with a pinch of salt. Had I not read Western analyses of these problems that dismantle these definite identities of Bamar or Padaung or whatever then I may have taken sides. I don't think these hostilities will die down because it's a good way for the government to hide its own weaknesses.

Late Morning

ေနတက်ချိန်

BDTZ

10283

Ma Thanegi
On The Burmese Character

Ma Thanegi is a jack of many trades — a Yangon-based painter and author, a one-time personal assistant to Aung San Suu Kyi, for which she spent three years in prison. Her books, which include her prison memoirs, *Nor Iron Bars A Cage*, and an account of her voyage down the length of the Irrawaddy River, *Defiled on the Ayeyarwaddy*, are marked by a sharp wit and adeptness at picking out the quirks and characters of Burmese society.

Your writing seems to reflect a continual amusement and intrigue at your country and people.

Oh yes, I'm always amused by the conversations of the Burmese. I am a local so I can eavesdrop and learn or overhear a great deal and it's usually quirky or hilarious. The people are full of humor and are constantly teasing each other (apart from the grumpy or self-pitying ones) so there's a lot of laughs even among the poor, especially the rural poor. We can laugh at ourselves in our poverty and hardship. It's not like we go around holding up hands in prayer as so many first time visitors have exclaimed to me, in complete amazement.

Visitors often remark about that magic hour in Yangon in the early morning, when the city quietly cranks into gear and the light is calm.

The days here start slowly with grey misty dawns and then comes more light, and almost all of a sudden — rush rush rush — people filling the streets, buses, and street bazaars and pavement shops (plastic sheets on the ground) over-spilling with piles of fresh luscious vegetables, fruits, meats, tons of fish. Small roadside stalls with boiling pots of soup for Mohinga noodles or gigantic woks of fried rice: breakfasts of champions. Most hawkers are poor but they're not mired in misery; they call out to customers, talk loudly to each other, tease, and joke. The day begins loudly and in the evenings, they are tired out, and with long waits at bus stops they are silent. In the evening Myanmar families like to stay cozy at home because with work and school, dinner is often the only quality time the family members can enjoy with each other.

The ritual of eating holds tremendous importance in Burma.

Food is important because its sharing is an integral part of relationships among the family, friends, neighbors, the community and so on. By family I mean a very extended one that would include blood kin of one's in-laws or cousins seven times removed. Long-standing neighboring families are also considered kin 'neighbor-relatives' as the term goes. Feasts to celebrate weddings, housewarmings, noviciation of sons and so on can have hundreds of guests. When I cook a nice dish, I send some to my neighbors and they do the same. When we travel we bring back foodstuffs from these regions not easily available in Yangon. Burmese love to eat too so that is why you cannot go two steps without seeing food on sale (and you cannot go a mile without seeing a pagoda.)

And the teashop? It's a veritable institution there.

Unemployed men sit the whole day in teashops discussing politics, poetry and women as no one drives them out and they can have endless refills of free green tea. Housewives do that too but usually do not sit in teashops — they are more careful with their money and there are too many men in teashops who might ogle them. Not more than that but we hate it. Ten years ago teashops had only tea and cakes but now they have meals of noodles or rice on the menu at reasonable prices so it's very convenient for workers or students, especially if they are single out-of-towners who live in private dorms rooms or rent a flat together. The teashops stay open from dawn to late in the night, so few single young people bother to cook at home. Under-aged boys work there and before righteous people start screaming, let me remind you they then have a place to sleep and food to eat. Unless their poverty can be addressed and solved, do not demand their dismissal.

How does spirit worship work its way into life here?

Buddhism is a very hard path to follow to the letter because there is no savior. You do bad things and it will come back to bite you in the next life, if not in this one. Buddhism already accepts spirits or celestial beings as 'creatures of the universe' so worshipping spirits fills this need of having favors granted, as do astrological rituals, but neither can remove the bigger bad karma of harm done to others. Spirit worship is more about pleasing them with ceremonies than fearing them. It's not about dark, evil worship, although even non-believers are careful about not angering them, which is why their shrines are protected — even Tree Spirits sometimes 'give' a dream in which he refuses to move, in which case a road is cut around it rather than the tree being felled.

Early Afternoon

မျိုးဆက်ကျောင်းသားများ

သတင်းစာရှင်းလင်းပွဲ

Ma Thida

ON THE BIRTH OF AN ACTIVIST

Ma Thida is one of Burma's best-known intellectuals, a physician, writer and activist who spent six years in jail in the 1990s, much of it in solitary confinement, for her support of Aung San Suu Kyi. She is the author of numerous books, including *The Roadmap* and *Sanchaung, Insein, Harvard*, a memoir of her early life, her years in the notorious Insein Prison and her time in the US. She remains an articulate and outspoken critic of the government, and is editor of the Pae Tin Tharn News journal.

You know first-hand the long-term psychological effects of military rule on the Burmese. This is something that could hinder society well into the future.

The first thing about long-term military rule is that it makes people fear one another, whether they are educated or not, rich or poor — it affects anyone. Anyone who opposed the regime felt this sense of fear and despair, and the close surveillance by the regime and the distrust it created was a very effective way of governing. This began in 1962, so after 50 years the community itself could not accept anything different — anyone who has different ideas to them, and so on. Self-censorship is still alive in thought, speech and deed. Because it has been risky to speak one's mind, people just echo the words of whoever has power and influence.

To what extent did your work in healthcare come to influence your political outlook?

I had been looking at all the poverty and it hit me hard. I would travel abroad a lot, and when I returned to my surgical ward after being abroad it was especially moving, unbearable, how the poor were suffering. They have no facilities, they don't really know their own rights — they thought they had none. I told them, "This is your body, this is your life, and based on the information I give you, please decide your own treatment." The way I practice is very strange for these people, because no other doctors ever gave them a choice — they told them what they needed.

So the healthcare profession in some ways mimics the regime's mentality.

It was very hierarchical. Doctors don't really know the democratic culture. They always asked for democracy, and I told them, "You have to practice it yourself." That's why in my small operating theatre I used to practice a democratic culture among doctors and patients, and after a couple of years they were happy with that.

Did one experience in particular ring alarm bells for you?

I was here during Cyclone Nargis in 2008 [which killed some 140,000 people] so I led a medical team down into the Irrawaddy delta and went around the camps giving treatment and health education. Afterwards I went to Brown University [in the US] on a fellowship and they asked what I'd learned from the experience, and I told them that the people of the delta suffered from a chronic syndrome of being ignored. That was my diagnosis. No one learned health care at school, so many children were anemic and had worms; sanitation was poor because they used the river as a toilet, but also for cooking and cleaning. And you couldn't believe it — so many patients turned up and when I asked what they were suffering from, they said nothing. "So why are you here?" "Oh, we had a headache, five months ago." It was so strange. So I asked again, "Why did you come to see me?" They said, "In our lives, we've never seen a doctor before." It was terrible, and that drove my activism.

That activism had earlier landed you with a six-year jail term. How did you survive?

In prison I would practice meditation for up to 20 hours a day. The way I look at myself and the universe has been dramatically changed because of the meditation. A lot of prisoners would meditate — it's like their exercise. To be a real Buddhist we need to have morality and our own wisdom, not learned from books or from monks. I feel this sense of impermanence, and that's why I feel very indifferent about whatever comes at me.

The government has released thousands of political prisoners since it came to power in 2011. Adjusting back into society must be a painful process.

In the past this sense of fear made the community discriminate against political prisoners and their family members. This had a powerful influence over their ability to deal with others who were often reluctant to develop relations with released activists. For some, this meant that upon release they became very anti-social and could not find a well-paid job. This would cause deterioration in their health and well-being. So many political prisoners died not only because of imprisonment-related health problems, but also because of socioeconomic problems born of discrimination.

Do you feel that things are changing for the better now?

It's not so straightforward. Nowadays, there might be a little more budget for health care, for instance, but there's no plan — all they want to do with this extra budget is finish using it, so they might build a new toilet or water tank, something very big and bold to show off, but no plan for how to use it for the benefit of society. For women, they are in some ways achieving better representation — many women's groups have emerged, and women are joining in advocating for their rights and protection of others'. But in rural areas, many young women are still cut off from these developments and don't know their rights at all.

You are a writer too. Was the regime effective in stifling creativity in literature and the arts, or did censorship actually fuel creativity and imagination?

It works both ways. We used a lot of tactics to overcome censorship, but on the other hand, we could not think things directly. That's the worst thing. There was no private news media; it was all government-owned. So in the past all the creative writers — novelists, short story writers, poets — had two jobs: one is to be creative for the sake of the beauty of language, and the other was to put information into their writing — because there was no independent media, they needed to play the role of journalists. Now however, people sometimes find it difficult to differentiate between journalism and literature: people expect to read between the lines — they don't ever believe the lines in the print, they just believe what they think is happening behind it.

Late Afternoon

မွန်းလွဲ

117

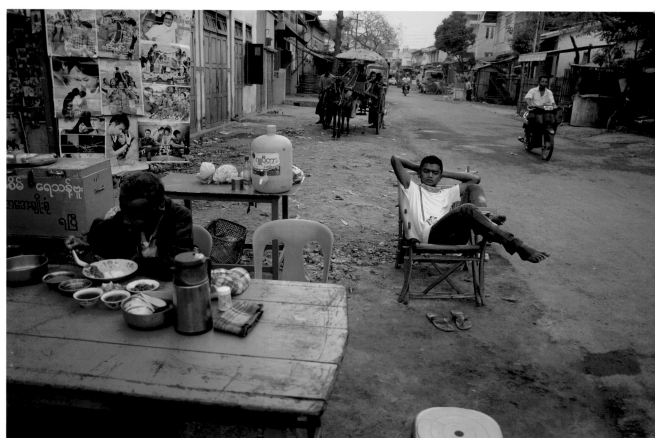

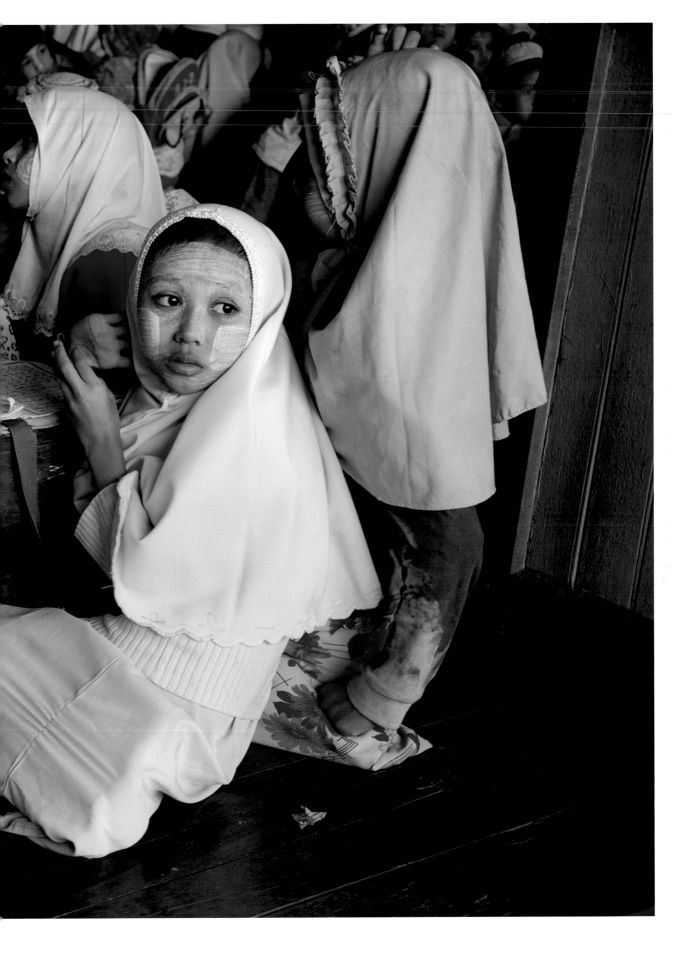

U Gambira
On Buddhism and Politics

U Gambira was at the vanguard of the 2007 monk-led uprising. The former head of the All Burma Monks Alliance, he was sentenced in 2008 to 68 years in prison for his lead role in the protests, and became an internationally recognized prisoner of conscience. He was released under a general amnesty in 2012, having suffered heavy and prolonged torture, the trauma of which remains. Upon being freed he was banned from re-entering monkhood and forced to seek medical treatment abroad.

Buddhism has been integral to the shaping of modern-day Burma, on a social and spiritual level, as well as a political one.

Buddhism has played a leading role in literature and education throughout the history of modern Burma. Before the British occupation [beginning 1824] the country relied entirely upon monastery schooling: the King, his commanders and counsellors, writers and poets, merchants, the poor—all of them were graduates from monastery schools, which is why Buddhist monks are addressed as *Sayadaw*, *Sayalay* and *Sayagyi* — *Saya* means 'teacher'. Although not as prominent as in the past, monastery schooling is still a very common source of education in Burma today. Up to a thousand years after Buddha's passing, Ari Buddhism had been the only sect of Buddhism dominant in ancient Burma. But they were ousted in the early Bagan dynasty era by the Theravada reform, led by King Anawrahta and Shin Arahan, and Theravada has since been the most prominent religion in Burma.

Monks have often taken on roles of political activists — the Panthaku monk who turned over his alms bowl, which signals that he refuses to accept a donation, to protest a Bagan king who coerced people into forced labour (NB: the Burmese word for boycott, strike and protest — *Thabeik Hmauk* — literally translates as 'turn over the alms bowl'); Shin Dithapamoukka, who led the peace mission to the court of Kublai Khan during the fall of the Bagan Kingdom, preventing Burma from becoming a Chinese colony; U Ottama, who fomented the nationalist movement in the 1920s against British rule, and Buddhist monks in the 1988 uprising and the 2007 Saffron Revolution.

More recently, religious tensions in Burma, particularly between Buddhists and Muslims, have spiralled into violence, with some monks taking a lead role in pushing anti-Muslim sentiment.

Some prominent monks have been preaching extremism and racism in an effort to dominate other religions. It's sad — what they are preaching is against Buddha's teachings and human rights. Much has to do with marriage between faiths. Their reasoning is based on a presumption that when Muslim men in Burma marry Burmese women, they coerce them into converting to Islam and so the law is necessary for preservation of Buddhism. The core problem is that there is no democracy in the country — our government is not elected by the people [the 2010 elections brought accusations of widespread vote-rigging and coercion]. Whilst trying to achieve democracy we should not discriminate against people on the grounds that they are Muslim, Hindu, Christian, Animist and so on. In the past we didn't — Muslims have been part of every revolution in every era, as were Christians and so on.

Has the government stoked these tensions deliberately?

If we can see everyone as just Burmese, just as the people, then all problems will be solved, but the military dictators have made it otherwise. They have divided people based upon religion and race so that they can justify their style of rule. In real revolutions we never differentiated between people based on their religion. But the government has no courage, and I will not forgive them for their crimes. Some, including Daw Aung San Suu Kyi, have said they will forgive but not forget. As for me, I don't forgive them — they have to receive judgement under the same laws that Pinochet in Chile and Milosevic in Kosovo and Pol Pot in Cambodia received.

You were subject to horrific torture in prison.

For the eleven months between my arrest in November 2007 and sentencing I was kept in solitary confinement in a 12-by-8 foot cell with no outdoor time. Then I was taken to the special courthouse inside Insein Prison in Yangon where the public and media are not allowed. I was sentenced to 68 years in prison under seventeen charges, and then transferred to Mandalay Prison. They also kept me in solitary confinement there, but it was worse this time because there was no one in the cells next to mine. I was all by myself in the wing and suffering health problems. There were groups of four interrogators taking turns every two hours asking me questions and threatening me. The poor food and the fact I had to sleep on a cement floor worsened my health. I then got transferred to Hkamti prison [in Sagaing division] and was again placed in solitary. I argued with the guards and so they took away my bedstead, food and everything — I was left in this empty cell on the cement floor, handcuffed behind in the back and legs shackled, and they would often beat me with a hood over my head. As I was handcuffed, I couldn't use my hands to eat so they assigned four criminal prisoners to come and spoon-feed me every day.

Other prisoners have talked about the power of meditation as a survival technique. Did you use this?

Meditation and exercise were important. Although my movement was limited by the handcuffs and the shackles, to the point where I could only sleep on my side, I would stretch my arms and jump up and down, which left me with this scar on my ankle for the rest of my life from the chafing of the shackles. Also, singing helps a lot — music is important. Most songs out there are about love and relationships, but in my view, it depends on how you look at them. If you look at them from the Dharma point of view, then they are Dharma lessons — they can also be political if you look from the political point of view. So I started singing songs aloud, despite my status as a monk. I have been into music since I was young — I used to own a guitar. With this, I strived to keep my hopes and beliefs alive, and also my body.

Dusk

ခရည်းခတ

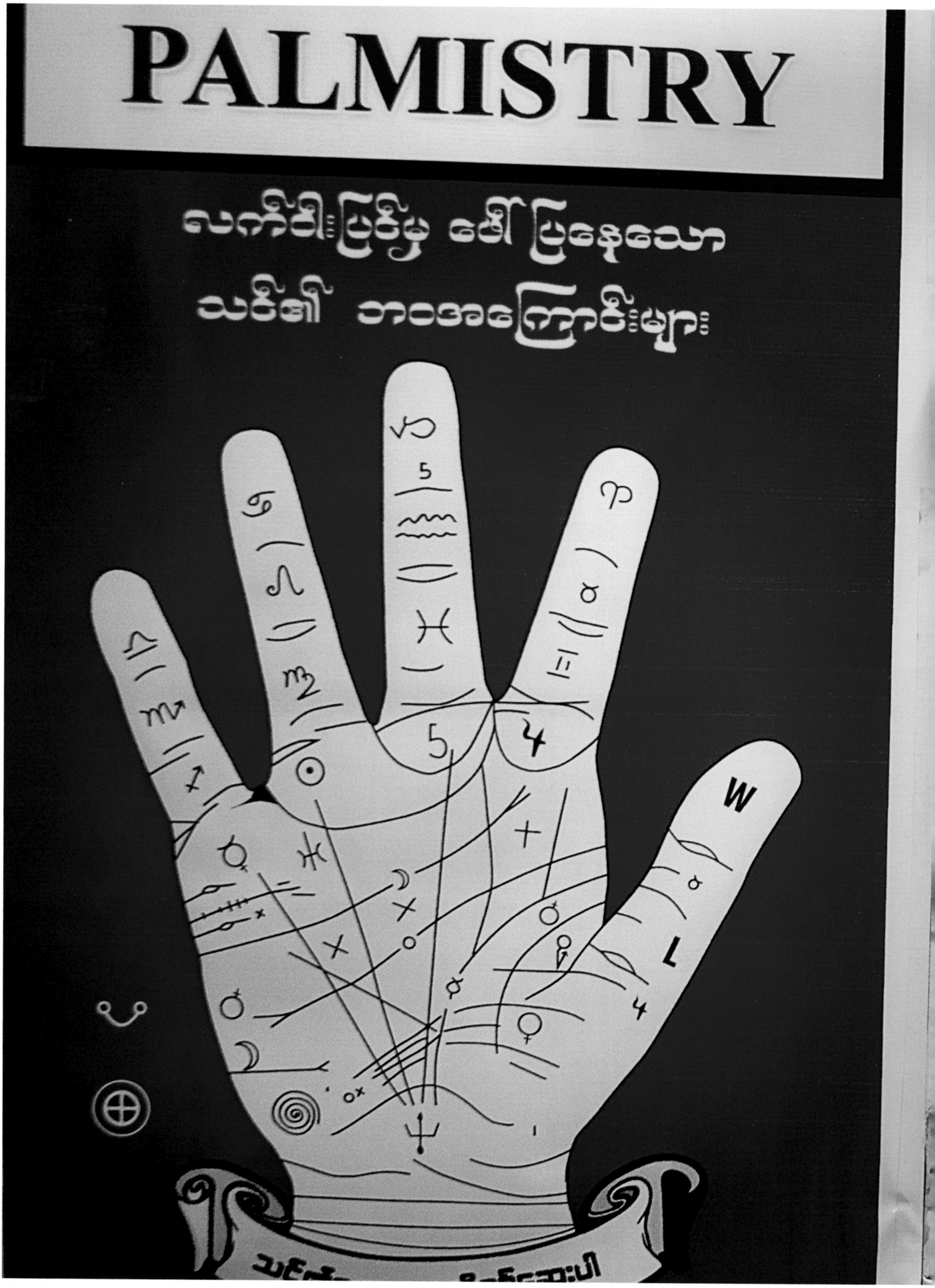
PALMISTRY
လက်ဝါးပြင်မှ ပေါ်ပြနေသော
သင်၏ ဘဝအကြောင်းများ
W
L

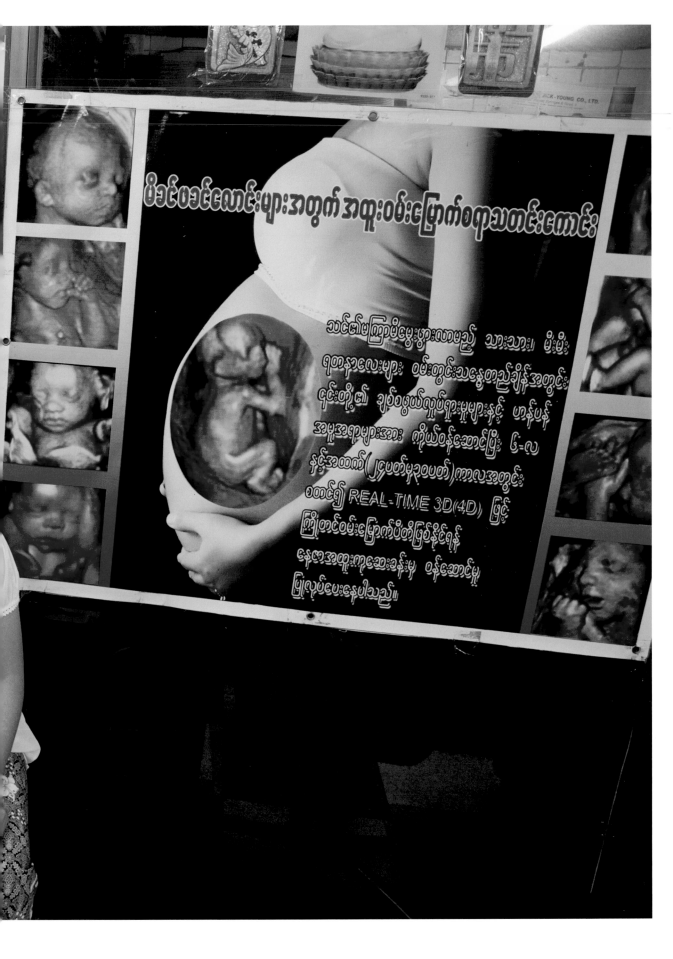

Nay Phone Latt

On Freedom of Speech

Nay Phone Latt rose to prominence during the 2007 monk-led uprising, or Saffron Revolution, when his blog served as a key window into the evolution of the protests and the ensuing crackdown by the military. He was jailed in 2008 for 20 years, and released in 2012. He was a recipient of the PEN/Barbara Goldsmith Freedom to Write Award, and was selected by TIME Magazine in 2010 as one of the Top 100 Most Influential People in the World.

Salman Rushdie once called you 'the voice of a generation'. That must have given you a strong sense of responsibility and influence.

Being called 'the voice of a generation' was an honor for me. Around the time of the 2007 uprising, the young generation in Burma didn't have a voice. Journalists were locked up because the regime, its general and business cronies, had profited from all the wrongdoing in the country and didn't want the world to know about this. But we used blogging and the internet to fill this void and fight for freedom of expression. Many bloggers emerged at that time and we had a big audience around the world, given there were Burmese communities all over the place who had fled the military regime. So bloggers became the voice of this new generation of dissidents — I think Salman Rushdie used this phrase not only for me but for all Burmese bloggers at that time.

The power of media to document uprisings was exemplified with the Arab Spring. Did we get an early indicator of that in Burma in the 2007 protests?

Because of our work and the developments in information technology in Burma the world knew more about the 2007 uprising than they did the 1988 uprising [when up to 6,000 people were killed]. When the regime lied, like with the shooting of Japanese photojournalist [Kenji Nagai] by soldiers in 2007, we used internet cafes to tell the truth. That is why they sentenced me to 20 years and 6 months. The regime sought to make everyone who participated in the uprising illegal, and outlawed all means of communication — Gmail, satellites, radio without a license, internet cafes without a license, owning uncensored material, and so on. I opened an internet cafe without a license and there were police watching it pretty much constantly.

Did the failure of 2007 weigh heavily on you once you were jailed?

The 2007 uprising may not have achieved its goals, but it was an important turning point in Myanmar's history. It pressured the regime to move towards the transition. It was the bridge that connected the past and the present — the younger generation who missed the 1988 uprising learned more about the military regime from the 2007 uprising. During those years the situation inside the prison and outside wasn't so different because the whole country was like a prison, and all citizens had lost their freedom. For me, although they sent me to jail to deter my freedom of expression, I tried my best to raise my voice — they can detain my body but not my soul and my spirit. I believe that no one but yourself can limit the freedom of your soul. What you are doing is more important than where you are. Prison is like hell but as a famous monk once said, the hero can change hell to heaven.

It is like hell, but many say it's also like a university.

It is, but you learned so many things that you couldn't learn at Oxford or Cambridge. My narrow cell was like a small library and classroom. We political prisoners held classes in my cell; we learned English, we learned about globalization, politics and we shared our own opinions among one other. The prison made us stronger and more educated. There is no political prisoner who is so afraid of prison that they'll give up doing politics.

There's a growing awareness across the world about the importance of blogging as a force for change.

Bloggers and other youth interested in media are playing a big role in the move to democracy in Burma and they will continue to do so well into the future. The media is a key pillar supporting the nation and bloggers play the role of citizen journalists — they are like a bulb, and if there is a citizen journalist in one place they can illuminate it and wrongdoings will decrease.

When you walk the streets of Yangon do you get a sense from the people that they are confident things are moving in the right direction?

What we have to do urgently is to create a trust-building process between the current government and the people. Trust is missing. People don't want to collaborate with the government because it has not given a chance to individuals that the people already trust. According to the constitution, the military has the biggest role in the administration and so the future depends on the military's policy. In a real democratic country, the destiny of the people should depend on their desires. So we need to amend the 2008 constitution if we want a secure future.

Night

Acknowledgments

This book project could not have been realized without the help of so many loyal supporters. I am grateful to you, Kickstarter backers, not only for your contributions but also for your moral support and networking efforts.

Over the years many people helped make it possible for me to return to Burma to continue my photographic work. Thank you to Drake Weisert, Htin Aung Kyaw, Adrienne Nutzman, and the American Center in Yangon. I am proud of my photojournalism students, who are able to report openly for media outlets both Burmese and foreign, now that censorship has eased.

The expert advice of Doug Cosper and John Badgley has been indispensable. Thanks also to Mary Bisbee-Beek, Don Unrau, Paula Swart, Aithan Shapira, Bruce Lellman and Andrea Brown. And to Kathy Ward, and the Fulbright Program, for your belief in the power of visual diplomacy.

The Cincinnati Foto Fest and Barry Anderson were the first to exhibit the work in print form, and I appreciate their foresight. Fuji Cameras provided equipment and technical assistance.

Wendy Doremus offered both financial support and understanding of the value of publishing photography. Bill Biggart you still inspire me to photograph those who are oppressed.

Family and friends are too numerous to name, but I couldn't do it without any of you. Special gratitude goes to Barbara Hiller for her steadfast encouragement, to Martin Brown and Rhonda Bennon for their support, and especially to Earl Brown.

The Verve Photo Blog community of documentary photographers has been a constant source of inspiration.

This book is the result of a dedicated professional team: journalist Francis Wade returned to Burma to do interviews for the expanded project, and Linda Sladek provided editorial skills and invaluable insight throughout the project.

Finally, my appreciation goes out to the Burmese scholars and activists who agreed to contribute interviews: Ma Thida, Thant Mint U, Pascal Khoo Thwe, U Gambira, Nay Phone Latt, and Ma Thanegi. Your insights help tell the story behind the photographs.

Gratitude goes out to countless other Burmese who provided assistance over the years, and who were so generous with their time. Thank you to all of the people who allowed me to photograph them.

Bios

Geoffrey Hiller is a documentary photographer who has been published in the USA, Europe, and Japan in *Geo*, *Newsweek*, *Mother Jones*, the *New York Times*, and other news outlets such as NPR. He has completed dozens of photo essays in Asia, Latin America, Europe and West Africa and was on the staff of the Brazilian magazine *Revista Geografica* for two years. His award-winning multimedia projects about Vietnam, Eastern Europe, Ghana, Burma, and Brazil have earned recognition from Apple, *The Christian Science Monitor*, *The Washington Post* and *Photo District News*. Hiller was a Fulbright Scholar in Dhaka, Bangladesh in 2008 – 2009. Most recently he has been working as a photography trainer in Myanmar, Cambodia and Pakistan. He is currently the editor of the blog *Verve Photo: The New Breed of Documentary Photographer*. His home is in Portland, Oregon. Visit his website at www.hillerphoto.com.

Francis Wade is a journalist and analyst who began covering Burma in early 2009 for the Democratic Voice of Burma news organization. Over the years he has reported on ethnic conflicts in the border regions, the rise of anti-Muslim violence, and the democratization process, including Aung San Suu Kyi's entry to parliament. He has also reported from across South and Southeast Asia, and is a regular contributor to *TIME*, *The Guardian*, *Foreign Policy Magazine* and other leading international titles. He is currently based in London.

Daybreak in Myanmar
Photographs by Geoffrey Hiller

First edition

Text and cover design by Emily García, Cathemeral Press
Print and color management by iocolor, LLP Seattle
Printed in China

Softcover ISBN 978-0-9905588-7-3
Hardcover ISBN 978-0-9905588-8-0

Photographs copyright © 2014 Geoffrey Hiller
www.hillerphoto.com

Foreword and interviews by Francis Wade

Front cover: Circle line train in Yangon, 2011
Back cover: Shwedagon Pagoda in Yangon, 1987
TOC: Shop interior in Meiktila, 2013